# DESTROY

## DIGITAL MEDIA PLATFORM

HOW **COMPETITIVE STREAMING™**

LEVELS THE PLAYING FIELD FOR CREATIVES

*by*

## *Christopher Grant Sr.*

X™

competitive **streaming**™

SEVEN
FIDANS
PUBLISHING

**Books By This Author:**

YA Sci-Fantasy Book Series:

***Sons of Caasi: Battle for Time***
*Special Edition Pre-Release*

*Visit: SonsofCaasi.com*

*Hardcover*      *Paperback*

 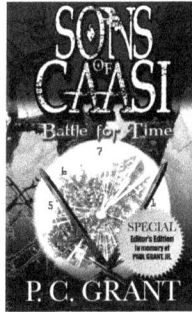

# COPYRIGHT

Sevenhorns Publishing
276 5th Avenue, Suite 704
New York, NY 10001
www.sevenhornspublishing.com

Sevenhorns Publishing is a division of SEVENHORNS.
The SEVENHORNS name and logo are trademarks of
SEVENHORNS, LLC.

Library of Congress Control Number: 2011914095
ISBN 9781736388792 (ebook)
ISBN: 979-8-9852007-0-6 (paperback)
ISBN: 979-8-9852007-1-3 (audio)
Printed in the United States of America.

# DEDICATION

*To Paul and Secnola Grant*
*Your love, unwavering support and commitment to the*
*vision surpass any earthly parental call*

*~*

*In loving memory of Paul Grant Jr.*

# TABLE OF CONTENTS

# ACKNOWLEDGMENTS

Special Thank You…

To my dear wife Tasha, daughter Sydnèe and son Chris Jr., my parents Secnola and Paul, my siblings Jennifer, and Paul Jr. (miss you, Bro).

It's difficult to mention everyone who has been a part of not just this book, but the vision behind it and so much more.

Love you all. Keep marching!

# ABOUT THE AUTHOR

Christopher Grant Sr.
SEVENHORNS *Founder & CEO*

Entertainment industry professional and author Christopher Grant, Sr. has over seventeen years of successful experience in the entertainment industry. As the founder and CEO of upstart media company SEVENHORNS, host of the DESTROY Podcast, and founder of TraxBox, Inc., Chris has recognized the power of multimedia to impact society for good. One of his lifelong pursuits has been to create and deliver culturally relevant content that will challenge the human condition.

His background includes several years in the trenches achieving gold and platinum level sales recognition for major artists like POD, Relient K,

Switchfoot, Skillet, DC Talk, CeCe Winans and others as the Northeast Sales & Marketing Territory Manger for CapitolRecords/CMG (formerly EMI/CMG), one of the world's largest music distributors. As VP of Marketing for an independent hip hop label distributed by Provident Music Group/Sony Music, Grant marketed and/or served as executive producer on several projects by Grammy nominated artists Lecrae, Da TRUTH, and The Cross Movement. He has also managed his son, Chris Grant Jr., whose credits include the voice of Tyrone on Nickelodeon's Emmy award-winning show The Backyardigans, and daughter Sydnée, who graduated from the USC School of Dramatic Arts in Los Angeles and plays Jess in the romantic comedy, "Accidentally in Love."

**Follow**

**Christopher Grant Sr.**

Linkedin: **www.linkedin.com/in/chrisgrantsr**
Twitter: **https://twitter.com/cgrantsr**
Facebook: **https://www.facebook.com/cgrantsr/**
Instagram: **https://www.instagram.com/cgrantsr/**

# URCs

## (UnderRepresented Creatives)

# PREFACE

The impact of digital media and its platforms has transformed the world. I've lived through the transitions from vinyl, to cassette, to CD, to downloading MP3s, to streaming. All the technological advances were welcomed and needed. Honestly, cassettes became a headache to deal with; sure, they were smaller than vinyl and easier to carry around, but I hated the tape it contained. It would always get caught up in my older brother Paul Jr.'s boom box. More often than not, I failed to pull the mangled tape from all the mechanical gears inside before he discovered the mess, and I'd get pounded.

Later, CDs arrived, but they had their issues, too. The darn things always got scratched, and kept skipping. I tried fixing the scratches with a pencil eraser, and using one of those CD cleaners, but I could never get the crazy thing to work.

The amazing MP3 changed the game. No more tangled tapes or scratched CDs! I could carry all my tunes on this cool device called an iPod. And MP3s only cost 99¢. I figured the low price was justified, since I had to pay so much for the iPod. I guess some perceived even that was too much. Soon, many of my friends downloaded tracks for free on a site called LimeWire. But I felt guilty going that route, as a producer and musician I understood the hard work we artists put in to our music, and deserved to be paid for it.

As a young boy, I made several homemade tracks with my older brother Paul, and I was inspired to make more after meeting legendary producer Maurice Starr (founder of New Edition and New Kids on the Block). I truly believed I would be the next Michael Jackson. I saved every penny I earned to buy equipment and spent endless hours honing my craft. I produced and sang songs in my basement as a teen with my best friend, Corey. Early on we called ourselves Chavè & Tysean, later we became Miragè. One highlight of our music career was performing at a pre-party for Milli Vanilli at The Pulse nightclub outside the Centrum in Worcester, MA.

We created several banging tracks — my brother concluded they were hits. He loved all our songs, even the ones that seemed strange. With an other-worldly musical mind; I know he was ahead of his time in that regard. For me, it was the greatest compliment that he called me "The Dean of Funk University." Following a couple of years of college, and with my brother as my biggest fan, it became time to take my career as a rapper/singer to the next level.

To make a long story short, my music career as a rapper/singer never made it to the next level. Like so many undiscovered indie artists, or underrepresented creatives (URCs), my career never took off. Over the years, I've often speculated about why. Was it the lyrics, the production, our looks, bad timing — or did we just suck?

Modern innovations like digital media platforms such as YouTube, Spotify, Amazon, and Twitter offer URCs a relatively cheap entry into the marketplace. They're no longer slaves to archaic formats like CDs, cassettes, DVDs, and printed books. The digital medium has little overhead and unlimited reach. URCs can now make their art available to billions of people around the world. We could reasonably restate "If you build it, they will come" to, "If you upload it, share it, or Tweet about it, they will listen, watch, read and buy it."

It would seem to follow that an artist who can make his or her content available everywhere might become the celebrity they've always dreamed of being — but that couldn't be further from the truth. I've written *DESTROY Digital Media Platforms: How Competitive Streaming™ Levels the Playing Field for Creatives* to share why millions of URC's will not reach the pinnacle of success in their particular field of creativity, and that it has little to do with their talent. Despite the unprecedented global reach of digital media platforms and the variety of content they offer, your content everywhere gets you nowhere.

Most digital media platforms aren't much more than digital photo albums to share with your family and friends — not springboards to stardom.

But, you ask, what about all the overnight sensations, the YouTube influencers, the videos, songs, and books that go viral? Sure it happens, but that's the exception rather than the rule. The platforms have brainwashed us into assuming going viral on digital media platforms is possible for everyone and the way to succeed as a creative. We're constantly fed this line of baloney, and it drives URCs to these platforms, hoping they'll be the exception.

By the end of this book, I will DESTROY much of what you think of digital media platforms and explain why they won't help you take your career to the next level, either.

But, don't worry. I won't leave you hanging. There is light at the end of the tunnel. I'll share with you why a concept I call Competitive Streaming™ is the future of digital media platforms and the key to unprecedented success for URCs looking to gain exposure for their content and earn a living from their creativity.

Although my expertise is in the entertainment industry, this book is for everyone, because we're all creatives at heart. *DESTROY Digital Media Platforms* is a must-read for artists, entrepreneurs, and anyone trying to gain traction for their brand in the world.

# INTRODUCTION

The need to DESTROY isn't always about getting rid of or demolishing things; in the context of this book, it is about shedding light on practices that need reassessment and invigoration for changing times. ***DESTROY*** *Digital Media Platforms: How Competitive Streaming™ Levels the Playing Field for Creatives* is the first in a series of DESTROY books that expose such things.

––––––––

We all are creatives. Those who are aware of it commonly refer to themselves as musicians, artists, writers, producers, or even entrepreneurs. We recognize household names like Taylor Swift, Steven Spielberg, J. K. Rowling, from music, film, and books, as well as luminaries in other industries in some measure because of their heightened ability to express their creative nature; but we have heard their names and are likely familiar with their work in some capacity because of the publicity they generate.

We all are creatives — so what about the rest of us? What about the unknown, underrepresented creatives? What about you?

Creatives no longer need deals with major companies, or brick-and-mortar retailers to share their creativity with the world. They increasingly are turning to digital media platforms like Spotify, YouTube, Netflix, Facebook, and countless others to showcase their creativity and try to make a name for themselves among "A-listers."

Retailers sell anyone's work online in the same stores as the stars. Take your shot at success and fame. Tell your friends, family, and anyone who will listen, "Hey, check me out! I'm on Spotify, Amazon, and YouTube!" Finally, you're validated. You're at the table with the big kids — Right? WRONG.

By introducing underrepresented creatives, or who he likes to call "URCs" to the groundbreaking concept of Competitive Streaming™, marketing and music industry insider Christopher Grant Sr. DESTROYs the idea that creatives must rely on traditional digital media platforms for discovery and levels the playing field for them to achieve success — regardless of fame, connections, or net worth. Grant DESTROYs commonly held myths about digital media platforms and what they do for URCs.

"I'm not here to bash traditional digital media platforms like Spotify, Netflix, and Amazon, etc. I love them and use them myself. But I know what they're good at, and what they're not good at. Unfortunately, one thing they're not good at is making you a star."

— Christopher Grant Sr.

# X

CHAPTER 1

# LEVELING THE PLAYING FIELD

The landscape of digital media entertainment is evolving at a breakneck pace. Music in particular, a top-heavy industry defined by it's A-list artists is now experiencing a semi-leveling of the playing field. A 2019 Rolling Stone article reports that "Over the past three years, the world's biggest artists have seen their market share of total streams — and therefore total money distributed by the likes of Spotify — decline significantly," and that "new artists, rather than older recordings, are gaining market share on audio streaming services; suggests something very important is going on in the global music business: A "middle tier" of new artists, operating away from the million-dollar advances of streaming's biggest acts, are increasing their share of the format's economics."

These findings signal positive change and bode well for that middle tier of new artists, but there is still more leveling to be done to positively impact the lower tier, or undiscovered artists. These acts struggle to get any leverage or exposure. Perhaps these undiscovered artists lack the talent necessary to warrant success, but I'd argue that there is always a diamond in the rough. Everything is liked by somebody.

In the not too distant past, it was next to impossible for an artist to record music at home without deep pockets. Now, with a little technical skill any artist can turn out a high quality recording. These recordings, even from undiscovered artists, deserve to be discovered. Of course, equal access and exposure doesn't equate to equal success, but the goal should be equal opportunity. That's what all creatives deserve — an opportunity to be discovered, regardless of finances, relationships, or even talent. Yes, talent.

Talent is defined as a special, natural ability or aptitude, the keyword being "special." And the perception of special ability or aptitude is highly subjective. Something considered special to one person might not be to others. Creatives are artistic; they demonstrate imaginative skill in some area or activity. We often perceive talent based on how it compares to something or someone already deemed talented. We say things like, so and so sounds like another artist who we already perceive as talented, but comparable perception isn't the sole determining factor of talent. Sometimes talent is expressed in stuff we've never seen before.

The music industry has been referred to as a copycat industry. Executives often seek artists whose skill sets have proven appeal, and they are hesitant to invest millions of dollars in artists they feel are too peculiar. They refer to those artists as unmarketable and risky. But, when we consider the artists that defined genres of music, their uniqueness and ability to break from the norm was key to making them household names. The white glove on Michael Jackson's hand was just one glimpse into his unique character as an artist. In a 2012 article for The Atlantic, Joseph Vogel, author of Man in the Music: The Creative Life and Work of Michael Jackson opined, "The hallmark of his art is fusion, the ability to stitch together disparate styles, genres and mediums to create something entirely new." From 1960 to 1970 the Beatles were like no other group. Each member brought his own character to the band as they evolved from 1950s rock & roll and Skiffle to pop ballads and psychedelic rock mixed with classical influences. These pioneers dared to buck the trends and launch into new territories, refusing to be chained by industry norms.

Many of the big names we love also had the fortune of being discovered and backed by major labels that promoted their artistry to the masses. This luxury is not afforded to most artists, and not always because they lack talent, but because the opportunity doesn't exist. What if the next Michael Jackson, Prince, Taylor Swift, Drake, or Beatles is out there, but they never get noticed because they cannot get a high-profile manager, make the connections, or find folk who believe in them? Maybe they're introverts who require the gift of gab. Creatives who maintain confidence in their creative skills but need marketing know-how and can only upload their art to a digital platform. Should these creatives be forgotten, destined to be buried in a digital haystack of data, forever? I say no. Everyone has some sort of talent. The key to success is finding and connecting with the people who value yours.

Digital media platforms allow creatives to connect with the people closest to them. They are great for sharing content through direct upload to social platforms like Twitter, Instagram, and Facebook, or subscription-based platforms like Netflix, Apple, and Spotify. The problem is that without paid advertising or celebrity status, these platforms do nothing to share content beyond your friends and family.

The playing field must be level for all creatives to share their content beyond their inner-circle. Changes in the entertainment industry resulted from advances in technology, such as going from CD/DVD to download and from downloading to streaming, but none of these advances has helped level the playing field for all creatives — until now.

Moving from traditional streaming to what I call Competitive Streaming™ will provide unprecedented opportunities for artists to gain exposure and grow their audiences. This is especially true for artists who are considered low-tier by current music industry standards. As technology continues its rapid advance, it's unclear what the digital world will look like in the near future. What is clear is the inequality among the classes of creatives occupying today's most prominent digital platforms and the challenges those platforms present for growing undiscovered artists' brands. The stage is set for Competitive Streaming™ technology to level the playing field for even low-tier artists or URCs to reach the world.

$$\overset{\displaystyle\widehat{\phantom{X}}}{X}_{\text{\tiny TM}}$$

CHAPTER 2
# MEDIA BIAS

Platform or publisher? This is the question of the day. Recent hearings brought the world's biggest tech giants — Google, Apple, Amazon, and Facebook to Capitol Hill to find answers to this question and others. We can describe a platform as a tech company that allows transmission and dissemination of information. "A good example is a phone company. When talking to a friend, certain words or ideas you communicate don't get censored or buzzed out. A platform is not responsible (legally) for the content posted."[1] A publisher is a company or person that acts as a custodian of content. For example, you can't just upload content and have it appear in the New York

Post. Someone must review it and assure it meets the paper's editorial standards and communicates a message that aligns with the paper's worldview. Publishers have the power to curate the content they publish so it aligns with their particular philosophy of life or conception of the world.

On May 28, 2020, President Donald J. Trump passed an Executive Order Preventing Online Censorship. Section 1 of the order states, "In a country that has long cherished the freedom of expression, we cannot allow a limited number of online platforms to handpick the speech that Americans may access and convey on the internet. This practice is fundamentally un-American and anti-democratic. When large, powerful social media companies censor opinions with which they disagree, they exercise a dangerous power. They cease functioning as passive bulletin boards, and ought to be viewed and treated as content creators."

Wikipedia, says "Censorship is the suppression of speech, public communication, or other information, because such material is considered objectionable, harmful, sensitive, or inconvenient (not suiting one's needs or purposes)." Governments, private institutions, and other controlling bodies can conduct censorship. The Executive Order on Preventing Online Censorship focuses on censorship of political views which run contrary to those held by a media platform's leadership, but the sentiment is transferable to all forms of public expression through online media. Communicating political views gives voice to an individual's ideas in the same way a song, book, or movie gives voice to the ideas, political or otherwise, of their creator. The only difference is the medium and manner by which we deliver the content. Ironically, the Executive Order Preventing Online Censorship has been rescinded and online platforms are once again free to act as gatekeepers.

The Communications Decency Act of 1996; Section 230 says, "No provider or user of an interactive computer service shall be treated as the publisher or speaker of any information provided by another information content provider" (47 U.S.C. § 230). This provision keeps services from being deemed a "publisher or speaker" of any content shared by its users. Section 230 (CDA) grants media platforms the benefit of sharing millions of tweets, posts, songs, and videos without fear of being convicted when objectionable content slips through the cracks. As a result, they are free from any liability when "in good faith," they cancel or tag user accounts or restrict and delete content they deem unacceptable. The editorial discretion they hold over users' posts, as well as over the content they digest allows digital media platforms to act as publishers — with the added privilege of being legally protected as a platform.

Digital media companies must decide who and what they are — platform or publisher. They can't claim to accept and publish all content but then show favoritism by excluding content they disagree with politically. Whether one agrees or disagrees with former President Donald Trump, he should have the right to communicate his opinions on an "open to all" social media platform as long as the material does not violate any of the sites clearly stated terms of use or privacy laws. The platform's rules must be applied fairly to all users regardless of race, gender, political leaning or societal status.

These biases are not only applied politically, but artistically as well when content is devalued by gatekeepers based on one's personal evaluation. It's like a phone operator deciding not to connect your call because they don't like the tone of your voice or the conversation you're having. On a platform all content should receive equal exposure.

Biases toward artistic content are not limited to social media platforms like Twitter, Facebook, or Instagram. Subscription platforms like Netflix,

Spotify, Apple Music, and Amazon receive content directly from aggregators or major distributors such as Warner, Sony, and Universal. Biases with these companies aren't as obvious, yet practiced on many levels. On the surface, these businesses should have the right to vet the content they deliver to their customers. We need and want them to do that for us, right? The problem here is that these major platforms control the narrative by pre-selecting the options we get to see or choose from. Sorta like going into an ice cream parlor where the owner only shows and serves chocolate and vanilla. Granted, it might be the best darn chocolate and vanilla ice cream in the world, but it's only chocolate and vanilla. What about all the other flavors, like pistachio, rum raisin, or strawberry? The ice cream parlor owner has removed the opportunity for you to taste hundreds of other flavors. You could always choose to spend your money at another ice cream shop, but with major content providers, not so much. Most of the media we consume is under the control of fewer than ten major media powers. These companies pre-determine what we see as hot and what's not.

The First Amendment to the United States Constitution specifically refers to the freedom of press and speech, but also extends to most expressions of art, including music, dance, film, literature, poetry, and the visual arts. Although its limitations apply to the government and not to privately owned media platforms, we must reevaluate and consider the sovereign power these platforms hold over free people — power not only to deliver but also to create, manipulate, and control the narrative of a society.

It's difficult to regulate the unique business model that digital media platforms represent in our country and around the world. A capitalistic free society offers near limitless opportunities for companies and industries to grow and succeed. Uncle Ben's admonishment to Spiderman still is true — "With great power comes great responsibility." Digital media platforms have a responsibility to the people who depend on them for the service they provide, including the duty to apply fair practices to all their users. And we should call out abuses of their power to forward particular agendas.

*1.* "Is Facebook a Platform or a Publisher?" Subsign.Medium.Com, Subsign.medium.com, 8 May 2018, Subsign.medium.com/is-Facebook-a-platform-or-a-publisher-f2e2fd04d4eb

CHAPTER 3

# YOU DON'T NEED THE INDUSTRY, YOU NEED AN AUDIENCE

"Life imitates Art far more than Art imitates Life."

— *Oscar Wilde, The Decay of Lying, 1889*

V ery little beauty is found in thick grey fog, but poet and playwright Oscar Wilde believed we can appreciate the beauty of fog in nature today because great painters revealed its beauty on canvas through their art. That world around us can be viewed in three ways. The way we believe it to be, the way we're told it is, and the way it actually is. Creatives have the power to show us the world as they see it through their creativity and art, their representations can be realistic or idealistic. Creatives wield not only the power to reflect the world around them, but also to create their version of it.

Billions of people around the world gather information about the people, places, and things around them from online digital media platforms. According to the Digital 2020 Global Overview Report, "More than 4.5 billion people now use the internet, while social media users have passed the 3.8 billion mark. Nearly 60 percent of the world's population is already online, and the latest trends suggest that more than half of the world's total population will use social media by the middle of (2020)." We can receive information via digital social media platforms as a tweet, song, book, or images. These mediums communicate something, but influencers, celebrities, and those who control the narrative can affect the way we perceive their messages.

For example, let's say you're indifferent about chocolate — you can do with or without it. Justin Bieber, your favorite artist, writes a song called "Yummy Chocolate." He invites his adoring fans to share why they love chocolate on social media, and to tag their posts "#I Love Chocolate." He sweetens the deal with the promise that 20 lucky fans will receive a "Yummy Chocolate" t-shirt. You reason, "I hate chocolate," (Remember, this is a hypothetical; I doubt anyone hates chocolate), "but I love the Beebs, so I participate for a chance to get and wear his gear." Justin Bieber just convinced you to represent something you couldn't care less about, just because you like him and his music. That's a loose example of how celebrities and/or influencers wield so much power in our society.

Never underestimate the power of influence. It can be good or bad, depending on the influencer. Most of us share similar preferences as the people we care about; we love the same things. It's been called human nature, herd mentality, groupthink, etc., but it's not always negative. Somebody's experience, review, or advice about a product, place, or thing keeps us from making mistakes and wasting our hard-earned money and time — effectively by allowing them to be our guinea pig. But, we miss some diamonds in the rough if we only try something new if someone else is speaking, tasting, wearing, or watching for us, even more so if we only ever do so at the urging of celebrities.

The celebrities and influencers we consider trend setters may not always be genuine. They, like us, are influenced as well; not only by other individuals, but by the big conglomerates that employ and promote them. This can be problematic in a way similar to the idea of Big Pharma partnering with the fast-food industry to raise funds for research to cure diseases caused by consuming fried and sugar-laden foods that drive prescription drug sales.

Influencers endorsing brands for profit not because they genuinely love or even actually use them is nothing new. That's just business. Celebrities advertise and promote brands all the time, right? We trust our influencers and celebrities to tell us what's good. Whether it's really what's good or just what's most profitable for them is hard to determine.

Digital media has made the world smaller and individual influence broader. Our pool of influencers — the people we look up to, follow, or emulate is no longer limited to societal A-listers. Now they include neighbors, friends, and family. Today everyone has access to the vehicle of influence that is social media. The number of people who follow us or our brand, dictates our power of influence. As a result, today's creatives have unprecedented power. They can build and reach an audience outside the means of the controlling media powers of BIG industry.

The power creatives wield as URCs are rarely tapped into, as many URCs continue to seek approval from the major companies in their particular industry to validate their God-given talents. They fail to realize that what they need is an audience, not the industry.

For many creatives, this is a difficult mindset to embrace. We're conditioned to the big household names like Sony, Warner Brothers, HBO, Netflix, and others. We conclude that unless we're repped by one of these major players; we haven't made it, and our talents are not worthy of the masses. This is a lie. YouTube, a platform built on the backs of URCs, has made thousands of people famous and financially secure — without the majors. URCs flock to the platform daily in hopes of building an audience and one day going viral. They are confident and assume they can be successful this way because they've seen others do it.

Going viral on YouTube is the exception rather than the norm, and many URCs find the possibility of virality as daunting as getting signed with a major. The obstacles to success and mainstream validation seem overwhelming with or without open-to-all platforms like YouTube.

URCs must ask themselves why they need validation from a major. At some point you should reason that if you like your stuff, maybe someone else will like it as well? Once again, the goal is to find people who like what you like and who value what you do. These people may or may not be the gatekeepers at some major company.

To find your audience, you need to know where to look — and it's not in the industry, which largely comprises of big money, suits, and copycats. Your audience is among the people, and the people are on digital media platforms. You need to get their attention.

$\widehat{\overset{\approx}{X}}$

CHAPTER 4
# DEATH OF THE GATEKEEPER

In the late 90s I worked in the music industry, selling music into brick and mortar retailers, specifically indie "mom and pop" stores, with a few larger chains sprinkled in. I would ask buyers to purchase a quantity of new releases based on historical sales, besides making sure they're well-stocked on the backlist or catalog titles. I pitched, sold in, promoted, and helped with sell-through.

Armed each month with the latest sales catalog featuring new releases from A list priority artists with the largest fan bases, or those whom the label invested a lot of money in, to what I call "C listers" or artists with smaller fan bases and smaller budgets. A-list artists occupied the first few pages of the catalog, and the top A-lister would occupy prime real-estate on the cover. Buyers seemed more than willing to meet or exceed their projections for titles featured in the front of the book. Your project placed in the front of the book meant the labels placed more marketing dollars behind you either as a household name, or new artists; therefore justifying the retailers bringing in larger quantities. The labels spent lots of money to drive music lovers to your store for these titles.

I loved selling music, but I always questioned whether consumers genuinely liked what I sold. I persuaded retailers to place music from A-listers front and center in their stores, but were A-listers I pushed really that much better than the C-listers? Maybe customers got sucked in, brainwashed because the artists' face is plastered everywhere? Could it be a song is played repeatedly on the radio, and they saw a CD on an end cap in the store with fancy verbiage and colors causing them to make an impulse buy. Something seemed wrong. Did people buy because they genuinely loved the music, or were they persuaded by marketing tactics? Do we like things organically, or do we like what we are told to like? And who's doing the telling?

The process of content going from creative to end-user can be complicated. Everything starts with an idea. Many of us have great ideas, but few move forward with them for various reasons. Lack of confidence, fear of failure, lack of support, or finances — creatives need tools. An idea is nothing without development and creation. For that, you'll need tools. Musicians need instruments, microphone, recording gear, etc. Film producers need a camera, and editing software. These days even writers need word processing software. Tools usually come at a cost, an aspect that might prevent one's efforts from ever getting started. People who overcome the initial hurdles might seek to validate a great idea through friends, family, and peers. All they need is for someone to say, "Hey, great idea," or "That sounds or looks amazing." People receiving positive feedback may eventually want to share those skills beyond their immediate circle of influence, and out to the masses.

Back then, when I was a sales rep in the music industry, it took a lot for an artist to make it to the people via the front cover of our catalog, if they even made it into our catalog. A lot has changed since those days. We've gone from CD's to mp3's and from music stores to streaming platforms. The one thing that hasn't changed much is the role of the gatekeeper, the person or entity that decides whether an artist is deemed A, B, or C-level. All your creativity and hard work could pass or fail based on the opinion of one individual or business entity is hard to accept. Unfortunately, that's how it's been for decades, and in many ways still is today.

Gatekeepers exist everywhere, and in every company. A gatekeeper's job is multifaceted. They must filter, define, promote, and present content they deem will bring financial profit, establish their company's brand, and satisfy the needs and desires of a target audience — or simply those of their boss! Consider the bouncer at a club, a secretary in an office, a buyer at a pawnshop, or a program director at a radio station — these people are usually the biggest obstacle between content and consumer.

In the entertainment industry, i.e. books, music, TV, and movies, gatekeepers are the conduit through which some of the greatest stories and music we've ever encountered has come. The ability of gatekeepers to spot diamonds in the rough has given us books like Harry Potter, The Hunger Games, and The Midnight Library. They've brought music from Lady Gaga, Drake, and Taylor Swift to the main stage. Gatekeepers have put the spotlight on movies like Star Wars, E.T., and Avengers End Game. Obviously, gatekeepers can be good at what they do. They're sort of like parents peeling the skin off an apple so their little ones can get right to the sweet, juicy part. Gatekeepers are a kind of filter for the people.

The music industry's primary gatekeepers are *The Big 3*: Sony Music, Universal Music Group, and Warner Music Group. Together they make up 68% of the music market. Three companies control over half the industry. These companies maintain relationships with key radio stations and disc jockeys around the country, and wield enormous power with other entities to ensure maximum positioning for their artists. These gatekeepers pretty much decide all the musical content we consume. We can say the same for the movie industry, where some of the same media conglomerates are in control. Warner Bros. Pictures, Walt Disney Studios, 20th Century Fox, Paramount Pictures, Universal Pictures, and Sony Pictures Entertainment account for over 50% of the market. And in the publishing industry Penguin/ Random House, Hachette Book Group, Harper

Collins, Simon and Schuster, and Macmillan dominate a significant share of their market as well.

Lots of great movies, songs, and books never see the light of day because they cannot gain traction or exposure. It's said that the cream always rises to the top, but shouldn't we question how much is skimmed off and thrown away because access is concentrated in the hands of a few industry execs?

Exclusion is often for necessary and obvious reasons, like keeping out offensive content. But some reasons for rejecting content are more subjective and screen out content based on political views or perceived lack of marketability, for example. Even technical standards can allow certain creatives in, while keeping others out.

A gatekeeper's censorship can be a two-edged sword for the consumer. In one sense they filter "trash" like offensive content so we don't have to. But beyond screening for offensive content, gatekeepers decide one man's trash is no man's treasure. What about the stuff we might have liked that gatekeepers end up rejecting? I guess one could reason that what we don't know won't hurt us, but I'd say it can't help us either.

Today's diverse online media landscape appears fertile and free of prejudice as creatives all over the world are encouraged to upload their media content to digital platforms, freeing them from the oppression and judgments imposed by traditional gatekeepers… but, not so fast — gatekeepers now show up in non-traditional ways on digital platforms. For instance, gatekeepers on digital media platforms can enforce rules like not monetizing creatives until they meet a particular threshold, or setting quality standards that determine whether content is even suitable for their platform.

Mega sites like YouTube are "open to all," yet success is largely unattainable for creatives without going viral, injecting major marketing dollars, or having longevity on the platform. Streaming media sites like Netflix, Spotify, and Amazon require an approved aggregator to deliver content to their platforms. Typically, you'll need to pay a small fee to use these aggregators. The fee just gets your content onto the various platforms along with everyone else's. With so much clutter, there's little hope of standing out. Your content everywhere gets you nowhere. So, while traditional gatekeepers seem absent on digital media platforms, creatives must overcome obstacles potentially more difficult than the censorship they employed.

Of course, anything worth achieving takes hard work, so I'm not saying getting discovered and being successful should be easy, but it shouldn't be impossible, either.

Do we really need gatekeepers? Sure, they seemingly make things a little easier for consumers, but don't you wonder what we're missing out on?

It's time for the death of the gatekeeper — time for we the people to decide what's hot and what's not.

# X

## CHAPTER 5
## NOBODY KNOWS ANYTHING

Willi022 Goldman, the Oscar-winning writer of screenplays for *All the President's Men* and *Butch Cassidy and the Sundance Kid* coined the phrase "Nobody knows anything," to refer to Hollywood producers who passed on future blockbusters. We could say the same today of those whose job is to predict the future of entertainment and digital media in a world where technology is advancing at breakneck speeds. Like the iPhone. The minute you feel the phone won't get any better, they release an update or a new one. Whether the update is minor or a technological game-changer, you see it's coming, and if you're addicted to technology like me, you're making the purchase. Although, standing in long lines and waiting overnight is a bit much.

Merriam-Webster's dictionary defines knowledge as "the fact or condition of knowing something with familiarity gained through experience or association." Professors get paid well to share their knowledge with our youngest and brightest. They write textbooks and give lectures on their knowledge and experience to impart to future generations. This is how society moves forward. Like a relay race where the baton of knowledge is passed from one generation to the next, and so on.

Wisdom is a word similar in concept, that the same dictionary defines as "the ability to discern inner qualities and relationships, or insight." Knowledge and wisdom are related, but not synonymous. Knowledge can exist without wisdom, but not vice-versa. You can be knowledgeable without being wise. Knowing how to use a pistol is one thing; wisdom is knowing when to use it and when to keep it holstered. In the past, younger generations welcomed the handing off of the baton of knowledge and wisdom. They often waited patiently in their symbolic 20-meter exchange zone. But modern technology allows the next generation to run out of the exchange zone, daring to venture into the future without the baton — the knowledge and wisdom of previous generations. Ironically, their zeal makes it difficult to sync up and make a smooth exchange between past and future.

Innovation and change seems to happen too fast to be captured in a textbook — not even a digital one — or fully grasped and understood by educators, let alone taught to students eager to push beyond the limits of historical norms. Educators who cannot grasp technological advances, the latest trends, and URCs who just think differently will become irrelevant in the future. Those responsible for educating and inspiring the next generation of creatives must meet them where they are. They must teach them the paths that have already been laid, so they can create their own.

I tell young people all the time that if anyone tells you they know all about digital media and the entertainment industry, they're lying — because it just changed again.

Wisdom is the ability to assess what's hot now, and use the knowledge to get a sense of what might be hot next. The best gatekeepers and industry leaders go beyond the norms in music, movies, books, etc., but doing so is risky. Most are reluctant to take the risk, choosing instead to rely on the copycat strategy for continued success. This strategy plagues the media industry and keeps most URCs undiscovered.

Did you know in 1977 Universal, Disney, and UA all passed on the *Star Wars* script? Top Hollywood studios rejected the 1981 *Back to the Future* script over 40 times before becoming the highest-grossing movie in 1985. No one would sign Kanye West, but he got a chance as an in-house producer. Then Roc-a-Fella Records reluctantly signed him. J. K.

Rowling once an unemployed, single mother on welfare sent her first Harry Potter manuscript to 12 different publishers, only to be rejected by all of them. She now has sold over 500 million books and is worth more than $1 billion. These are just a few examples of overlooked talented people. Search the net; you'll be shocked at how many great creatives were passed on because they didn't fit what someone thought would sell.

We can't predict someone's future success, but here are a few things that these initially overlooked creatives had in common:

- They believed their creativity was worth sharing.
- They took the first step.
- They never gave up.

Someone once said, "Nothing beats a failure but a try." As a URC, don't be discouraged because the mountain of success seems impossible to climb. Don't reason that gaining an audience and earning a living through your artistry is a fantasy. Don't talk yourself out of trying.

Fortunately, the rules of stardom are changing. Financial barriers are being broken down for expressing one's creativity through music, movies, books, acting, etc. The tools of creation are more accessible than ever. Social media platforms allow you to deliver content digitally to countless people without the cost of physical manufacturing. No one can stop you from putting your content out independently — whether they like it, or not.

Creatives no longer need validation from third parties, big or small. You can make and put just about anything out. The problem is getting eyes on your content, if you can get eyes on your content, odds are somebody in the world will like it. Why, you ask? Well, because you like it. Although we all are unique creatures, there are certain traits, or preferences groups of us share in common. For example, think of words. They can vary in meaning, but they all have letters in common. The words m**us**ic and tr**us**t are two different words with entirely different meanings, but they have "**us**" in common. They share this connection on a deeper than surface level. Creatives need to find the audience that connects with their creativity on that deeper, less obvious level. This might not be the best example, but I hope you get my point.

In our modern, fast-paced world, we've become accustomed to looking at the surface and not much deeper, especially for those who entertain us. We've been brainwashed to focus on and judge creatives by their exterior appearance, who they're connected to, or what others say about them without ever really connecting with them around their artistry. Favorably for URCs, social media is allowing (forcing?) creatives to more intimately connect with and grow their audiences.

Sure, most digital media platforms and their tools continue to favor established celebrities, but the fact that nobody knows anything should create a sense of optimism among today's URCs. Now, anyone can enter the creative arena. And no one can say you're not good enough because nobody knows anything.

$$\overset{\displaystyle\frown}{X}$$

## CHAPTER 6
# DESTROY

My experience in the entertainment industry has afforded me a unique perspective on the ins and outs of the industry and how it works as it relates to digital media and our consumption of it. Obviously, we have our pros and cons in any industry. The pros must be nurtured, and if possible approved upon. The cons, we must DESTROY.

The digital revolution has made the world smaller. Creatives could take months, if not years, to deliver his or her art (music, video, book, etc.) from conception to consumer. Now, with instant uploads to social media sites and platforms like YouTube, getting content out can take less than an hour, or at most a few weeks if delivered through an aggregator to sites like Netflix, Amazon, Spotify, or Hulu. In addition, tech companies like Apple, Blackmagic Design, Adobe, and many others have advanced the "prosumer" concept and market, making professional level tech more accessible to the amateur and blurring the lines between high and low-end equipment, so now you don't need deep pockets to make your art a high-quality reality. These days with plugins you can get the sound of a $50k SSL board (mixing console), or Neve 1073 (equalizer/preamp) sitting in your basement on your DAW instead of in a fancy, expensive studio. You can get video quality that some say rivals an $80k Arri from a camera costing 1/3 the price. These are just two examples among many of the possibilities for creatives to produce content that meets industry standards at less prohibitive costs.

Innovation can be great, but we commonly see an unexpected downside, or seesaw effect where one side goes up, and another goes down. While the ability to reach consumers is much easier, the drawback is just that — it's too easy. Anyone and everyone can share their capabilities, regardless of skill, talent, or even the so-called "it factor." The sheer, unhindered droves of wanna-be creatives flocking to digital platforms like YouTube and others to share their content with the world is astronomical. YouTube has over two billion users. The amount of content on the platform is overwhelming, and trying to get noticed amid so much media can be daunting. Everyone wants to be an influencer, and it can be impossible to stand out from the pack.

If you're brave enough to enter the clutter, you face the uphill battle of gaining exposure by amassing likes, follows, shares, mentions, etc. hoping to go viral, which is not likely to happen on your journey up the mountain toward digital media fame. Many creatives optimistically still dare to climb. According to a Stanford University study, less than 1% of content goes viral; and only one Tweet in a million goes viral. Most content consumed on social media is posted by celebrities who are already famous. I hate to be the bearer of more bad news, but the reality is that most upstart creatives who rely on social media to gain a following and exposure are likely to fail.

Perhaps you're a musician whose part of that 1%. You go viral, or at least gain significant traction through friends, family and tons of fans who think you're just cool as heck. They shower you with likes, follows, shares, @mentions, reTweets — all that. Now, you might begin asking yourself a few questions, like:

- Will this translate into actual wealth?
- Could I eventually quit my day job and make a living doing this?
- Will people who like me today continue to like me and pay for my art?

For most of us, music is priceless. Songs remind us of our first wedding dance, a high school weekend jam, special times with family and friends, and countless moments experienced over the course of our lives. Music has so much meaning and value — yet no one seems willing to pay a fair price for it.

The devaluation of music has discouraged many artists, who often quit making music altogether because of unfair compensation, or what we commonly referred to as "the value gap." Put simply, the value gap describes the overwhelming discrepancy between the amount of music consumed and the profits paid out to the rights holders. Most music is stolen or consumed on YouTube for a fraction of a penny. For example, YouTube pays out an average of $0.00069 per stream, so you would need a minimum of 2.1 million streams to earn a minimum wage in 2020. With a catalog of 35 million songs, Spotify pays out just $0.00437 per stream, and that amount decreases even more as the site grows.

Without a doubt, digital media platforms are one of the most significant innovations of our time. Their influence on the world, be it via music, movies, or books, cannot be underestimated. It can't be said often enough, "With great power comes great responsibility." Despite the positives, one cannot ignore the areas in need of significant improvement.

We live in a time when the capacity to share creative expression and artistry is at an all-time high, yet digital media platforms have a stranglehold on the ability of URCs to get paid and gain exposure. The barriers between URCs and the multitude must be removed. Third-party validation of artistic creativity should and will be a thing of the past, but eliminating these barriers will not be easy. Doing so will require traditional digital media platforms to remove practices that ultimately are their bread and butter.

Open-to-all digital media platforms fall short of fairly and equally representing all participants, and often, URCs are the ones who are left out. They naïvely believe that if they supply their content to the plethora of digital media platforms, somehow the masses will be exposed to and consume their content. The possibility exists in theory, but it's not likely to be realized because, as mentioned earlier, the only people consuming URC content is a small audience of friends and family. The time has long passed for these aspects of digital media platforms that make it difficult for URCs to succeed be DESTROYed.

$\widetilde{\mathrm{X}}$

CHAPTER 7
# COMPETITIVE STREAMING™

We live in a highly competitive society. Although modern opinion would suggest it's better to enjoy the game rather than compete for the prize, human nature drives us to win and be better than the next person. Nobody wants to lose. Workers compete for the best jobs. Athletes compete to be champions. Retailers compete for our dollars — the list goes on and on. Competition can be a good thing and a key to a fair marketplace, democracy, and cultural growth.

This is an exciting time of fluidity and permutation. Mega tech startups like Facebook, Spotify, Amazon, and many others leave entrepreneurs, creatives, and society in a constant state of creativity and expectation. Everyone is looking for the next big tech startup. Products and services must get faster, easier and cheaper, be more innovative, and just plan better than before. In this fast-paced modern environment, no one can remain content because contentment leads to stagnation. Stagnation leads to falling behind and, eventually, failure.

So what is the next big thing? Nobody knows for sure. What we know is that most world-changing innovations and tech empires were birthed from an obvious and necessary need or desire. Ultimately, we all want things that make life a little better.

The transition from CDs to music streaming platforms has made music more accessible. No more waiting for weekly episodes on network TV. Now we can binge an entire season in a weekend on streaming platforms like Netflix. We can view what we want, when we want. Listening to audiobooks lets us enjoy entire books, sometimes on a single road trip. These kinds of innovations have affected us all, and what they have in common is that they came to us via a digital media platform. So, it wouldn't be a stretch to speculate that the next big tech innovation might also involve digital media platforms — and I believe that the next big world-changing tech innovation is Competitive Streaming™

Competitive Streaming™ solves three primary problems that have plagued creatives seeking to gain exposure for their content on traditional digital media platforms: Clutter, Value, and Exposure. I'll focus specifically on these problems as they relate to URCs (underrepresented creatives) because I understand URCs drive content creation. To solve the biggest issues with traditional digital media platforms for them will also clear up problems for their audiences, i.e. consumers of their content.

One of the first major hurdles URCs face on traditional digital media platforms is clutter. There's just too much content for them to get noticed. Exposure and building a paying audience by going viral is a pipe dream. Sure it happens, but it's not likely.

Many digital media platforms employ complex algorithms to prioritize content as high quality and relevant based on constantly changing factors that make it difficult to gain positioning. Most people can't decipher these algorithms with any consistency, and so must resort to reaching people organically, or by purchasing ads, which bodes well for the platform as more revenue is driven their way.

A second big challenge URCs face on traditional digital media platforms is the devaluation of content. The money stolen or kept from music artists is well documented. But the devaluing of content happens not only with music. Digital content everywhere is devalued as a result of lower overhead for production, packaging, and distribution. Although A-listers are still likely to be paid big bucks whether their content is seen on Netflix or the big screen.

And finally, a third major challenge URCs must overcome on traditional streaming digital media platforms is exposure. As I've pointed out, if nobody knows who you are, your content everywhere gets you nowhere. So what if your music is on Spotify, Apple, and Amazon? So what if your new indie film is on Netflix, Amazon, and YouTube? So what if your indie book is on Barnes & Noble Nook, or Amazon KDP? Nobody knows or cares! Well, your friends and family might — but that won't pay the bills.

Despite these seemingly insurmountable obstacles, URCs keep pursuing their dreams. We live in a world of creatives. On traditional streaming digital media platforms, URCs are developing most of the content that no one is seeing. Competitive

Streaming™ allows URCs to get their content in front of the masses who value and consume it.

## What is Competitive Streaming™?

Creatives have long been in search of a platform that will allow them to rise above the clutter, gain exposure, and earn a consistent, livable income from their art. While many streaming platforms today offer tools, programs, and initiatives such as paid advertising, paid playlist placements, and long shot playlist pitches, URCs find themselves disillusioned as these devices cannot meet their needs. Temporary spikes in streams, views, and follows fade, with no long-lasting hope for success.

I believe the concept and implementation of Competitive Streaming™ will finally meet the expressed needs of URCs in a single, innovative platform.

Competitive Streaming™ is media streaming driven by a system that allows users to control how content is ranked, valued, and publicized within a digital community. Users voice their opinion on digitally streamed content directly by election, and indirectly via aggregated mentions shared in a self-contained social media platform.

## Competitive Streaming™ Solves the Problems

**CLUTTER:** *Competitive Streaming™ Gives You No Clutter, Just The Best Content in The World*

When I was young, many radio stations would feature a battle of the bands. They would play two new songs back-to-back, then have listeners call in to vote on which song should stay and which should get booted. The artists featured in the battle were usually newly signed to a major label. I remember running to the radio to listen to these battles so I could record the songs and be the first to hear and share the hottest new music.

The battles were competitive, and I loved it. Competitive Streaming™ cuts down the clutter by allowing the people to choose what's hot and what's not, instead of industry gatekeepers or third party influences. Users preview snippets of new material and choose to elect it or reject it. Rejected content is removed from that user's feed, thereby eliminating clutter. Content rejected by one user may be elected by others. Content with the most elections makes up the best content in the world, according to the people in the world — not the industry.

**VALUE:** *Stop Paying for Billy Bob's Lambo*

Billy Bob is that artist you don't listen to, but every time you pay your subscription fee on sites like Spotify, you're footing the bill for his luxurious lifestyle. You might be in love with alternative inspirational pop artist Marcus Akeem Bradley, but Marcus Akeem Bradley's market share represents a microscopic cut of Spotify's billion streams each month. So the majority of your $9.99 monthly subscription fee pays Billy Bob — or whoever is getting the lion's share of Spotify streams. Competitive Streaming™ lets your money directly support the creatives you consume.

Platforms like Spotify use a payment model called stream share. That means they pay artists based on the artists' share of total streams on the platform. This does not bode well for URCs, whose cut is usually next to nothing. To add insult to injury, that cut diminishes as more artists join the platform.

Competitive Streaming™ platforms use what I call a User Percentage Payout (UPP) model. This model allows creatives to get paid based on their net share of each individual user's streams, as opposed to being paid on a percentage of total streams on the platform. We pay creatives from subscription fees of users who actually consume their content.

Imagine getting the net share of the subscription fee for every user who only consumes your content.

Competitive Streaming™ increases the odds of making a living from your art. Cha ching! Cha ching!

**EXPOSURE:** *Essentially, Everyone Consumes Everything in Their Selected Genre*

The rotation mechanism within a Competitive Streaming™ platform maximizes engagement by increasing impressions based on time on the platform (user-time). Your content stays in rotation until all users of a genre consume a preview of it. We expose your content to everyone who chooses your genre.

Competitive Streaming™ levels the playing field for creatives by eliminating third-party influence on content advancement. Organic interactions drive the system with content in real-time. The people are the algorithm. No more gaining exposure through back-door relationships or deep pocket investment — you can't pay to play on a Competitive Streaming™ platform.

You've probably experienced the hassle of skimming through hundreds of poor options generated by some mysterious algorithm for what to read, listen to, or watch. Like, you've spent more time scrolling through a menu of hundreds of channels you'd never watch than actually looking at something good. You've probably also had the satisfaction of checking out a recommendation from a friend on what's hot — or totally agreeing about what's not. Competitive Streaming™ doesn't stop filtering, it changes who's doing the filtering, from people in suits, to you. Again, the people are the algorithm.

Traditional digital media streaming platforms attempt to supply content they assume we like based on our previous selections or categories we select. The problem with this is that gatekeepers have already filtered content based on historical sales, celebrity, cash, or all of the above — before we see it.

I believe digital media platforms that regulate and separate users from content based on historical sales, celebrity, or cash driven agendas will soon give way to innovative, true, direct-to-user/consumer platforms that deliver content based primarily on user taste. This is the essence of Competitive Streaming™ — that the people will decide for themselves.

# Thank you for reading!

### DESTROY Digital Media Platforms
How **Competitive  Streaming™**
Levels The Playing Field for Creatives

If you enjoyed this book, I'd love for you to post a review on Amazon, Goodreads, BN.com and/or any site this book is sold.

# Partner With Us

## TraxBox
### Competitive Streaming™ platform

**TraxBox | Competitive Streaming™** levels the playing field for creatives by eliminating 3rd party influence on content advancement — you can't pay to play on TraxBox. If you're an investor, creative, or just a lover of music, movies and books, we need your support. Our platform is disruptive and will revolutionize the way we consume digital content. Like, all tech companies we need traction and money. Below we've listed several ways you can assist us and be a part of this groundbreaking platform.

# CONTRIBUTE

**competitive streaming**™

## CompetitiveStreaming.net
*Go here if you would like to make a financial contribution.*

## CREATORS:
## TraxBox.com
*Go here if you're a creative*

## USERS:
## TraxBox.com
*Go here if you LOVE ENTERTAINMENT MEDIA*

## MAILING LIST:
## ChristopherGrantSr.com
*JOIN MY MAILING LIST Let's Stay Connected*

## DESTROY Podcast

If you like this book, please check out DESTROY, the podcast that's helping creatives eliminate the barriers between them and the people.

*DESTROYPODCAST.com*